# Hippo Calves

Julie Murray

**abdobooks.com**

Published by Abdo Kids, a division of ABDO, P.O. Box 398166, Minneapolis, Minnesota 55439. Copyright © 2019 by Abdo Consulting Group, Inc. International copyrights reserved in all countries. No part of this book may be reproduced in any form without written permission from the publisher. Abdo Kids Junior™ is a trademark and logo of Abdo Kids.

Printed in the United States of America, North Mankato, Minnesota.

102018

012019

Photo Credits: Alamy, iStock, Minden Pictures, Shutterstock

Production Contributors: Teddy Borth, Jennie Forsberg, Grace Hansen

Design Contributors: Christina Doffing, Candice Keimig, Dorothy Toth

Library of Congress Control Number: 2018945725

Publisher's Cataloging-in-Publication Data

Names: Murray, Julie, author.
Title: Hippo calves / by Julie Murray.
Description: Minneapolis, Minnesota : Abdo Kids, 2019 | Series: Baby animals set 2 |
    Includes glossary, index and online resources (page 24).
Identifiers: ISBN 9781532181658 (lib. bdg.) | ISBN 9781532182631 (ebook) |
    ISBN 9781532183126 (Read-to-me ebook)
Subjects: LCSH: Hippopotamus--Juvenile literature. | Baby animals--Juvenile
    literature. | Zoo animals--Infancy--Juvenile literature.
Classification: DDC 599.635--dc23

# Table of Contents

Hippo Calves . . . . . . . .4

Watch a
Hippo Grow! . . . . . . .22

Glossary . . . . . . . . . . . .23

Index . . . . . . . . . . . . . .24

Abdo Kids Code . . . . .24

## Hippo Calves

A **female** hippo often has one calf at a time.

Most calves are born in water.

The calf is 3 feet (.9 m) long.

It weighs 100 pounds (45.4 kg)!

The calf comes up for air.

Its mother helps.

The calf is tired. It rides on its mother's back.

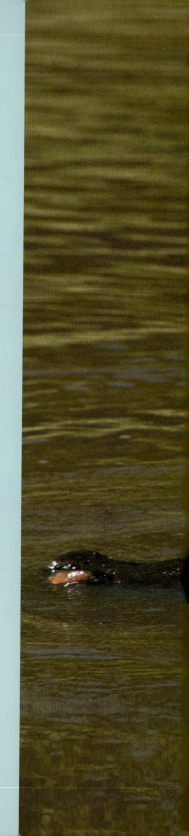

It drinks its mother's milk.

It soon will eat plants too.

The calf grows fast. It can **gain** 10 pounds (4.5 kg) a day!

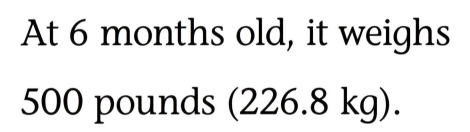

At 6 months old, it weighs 500 pounds (226.8 kg).

It plays with other calves.

They like to roll in the mud.

# Watch a Hippo Grow!

newborn

3 months

1 year

5 years

# Glossary

**female**
a girl animal that can have young.

**gain**
to take on as an increase.

# Index

breathing 10

food 14

growth 16, 18

mother 4, 10, 12, 14

movement 12

play 20

size 8, 16, 18

water 6, 10

Visit **abdokids.com** and use this code to access crafts, games, videos, and more!

Abdo Kids Code:
**BHK1658**